Do Disrupt

Change the status quo.
Or become it.

Mark Shayler

CHRONICLE BOOKS
SAN FRANCISCO

This book is dedicated to Nicola.
Yin to my Yang.
Squire to my Brown.
Egg to my bacon.
Gin to my tonic.
Paul to my John.
Ernie to my Eric.
Dandelion to my Burdock.
Vic to my Bob.
Marr to my Morrissey.
Love and Peace x

First published in the United States of America in 2018 by Chronicle Books LLC.
Originally published in the United Kingdom in 2013 by The Do Book Company.

Library of Congress Cataloging-in-Publication Data available.

ISBN: 978-1-4521-7145-6

Manufactured in China.

Cover design by James Victore.
Interior design by Anthony Oram.

10 9 8 7 6 5 4 3 2 1

Chronicle Books LLC
680 Second Street
San Francisco, California 94107

www.chroniclebooks.com

Contents

IF IT AIN'T BROKE

BREAK IT.

Tom Peters

Introduction

THIS BOOK IS ABOUT DISRUPTION.

It's about doing things differently. About having ideas that will change the world. That will at least change your world. It's also about delivering those ideas.

Having ideas is easy. The difficulty is making them work. Maybe you're hampered by issues of confidence, inertia, money, knowing where to start.

It's easier said than done, but you just need to start.

This workbook will help you create ideas and it will help you take those ideas from concept to customer. It'll help you do things differently. Hopefully it will make you happy.

WHAT IS DISRUP-TION?

Since the first edition of this book, the word "disrupt" has become overused. Every stalling or failing business talks about the need to disrupt. Every startup aims to disrupt the market. Every agency has a "process" for disruption (oh, the irony). While the word is overused, the application of disruptive creativity is still fairly rare. There are very few examples of companies who are truly embracing fast and disruptive ways of thinking.

Everyone points to companies like Uber and Tesla as examples of hyper-disruption. Uber is a common example, and many commentators argue that it isn't actually disruptive.* But Tesla is disruptive. Or, I should say, founder Elon Musk is disruptive. He is audacious and brave. Whether through solar roofs, mega batteries, Tesla, or SpaceX, his vision and embracing of new technology is genuinely disruptive. Indeed, he doesn't just harness technology, he pushes it farther than anyone else. But look closer to home for the most disruptive company around: Amazon. Everything it does is geared toward disrupting, even destroying, the markets of its competitors. CEO Jeff Bezos once said, "If you're going to invent, you're going to disrupt." Amazon is frighteningly good at disrupting markets. Obviously it started in books, then moved into e-readers (the Kindle wasn't developed to convert older readers to tech, it was developed so readers would never buy books from anywhere else), same-day delivery, Amazon Prime, Amazon Fire Phone, Amazon Music, Amazon Video, Amazon Fire TV, Amazon Studios, the Amazon Dash Button, Alexa and Echo, AmazonFresh, Amazon Go—and they've now acquired Whole Foods. The list is endless. Amazon is brilliant. It is frightening. What drives it is a desire to have a digital impact upon, and to improve upon, everything. This coupled with the company's small and agile teams means that it has both the power to change anything (literally anything), do it quickly, and watch it soar—or to be happy to have learned from the mistake and put the idea in the trash.

* Clay Christensen (Harvard Business School professor and originator of the term "disruptive innovation") argues that in order for a business to be disruptive, it must gain a foothold in a low-end market that had been ignored by the incumbent in favor of more profitable customers. Otherwise, the disruptor must create an entirely new market, turning noncustomers into customers. Uber doesn't fit into either of those boxes: It targets people who already use taxi services, and it doesn't provide a particularly low-end or cheap experience.

If you call yourself disruptive but don't do any of these things, it's mainly all hot air. It is wishful speaking. Saying your new product is disruptive doesn't make it so. Introducing a new flavor of ice cream, or a product that has slightly less sugar, isn't disruptive. It is simply a new flavor of ice cream or, in the second case, doing things less badly. This is just tinkering.

What is disruption? It's about changing the pace or direction of what you are doing. This applies to the individual as much as it applies to a company. This latest edition of the book you are holding has a whole new section on how to be disruptive inside a large organization—helpful because not everyone wants to, or is in a position to, launch a startup.

There are consequences of disruption, however. You can't just go around creating mayhem for the sake of it. It has to be purposeful. There has to be a purpose, because with disruption comes responsibility. Here is a story to illustrate this point.

When I was around ten I became dissatisfied with the quality of school lunches. This was the 1970s and food everywhere else had become exciting. It was all convenience and speed, even at the expense of nutrition. But food at school was still pretty wholesome and good for you. We didn't want this— we wanted to be able to bring more interesting food from home. We wanted sandwiches full of cheese and prawn spread (yep, really, and it still exists). We wanted pickled onion–flavored chips, chocolate bars, overly sweetened yogurt. We wanted bad food at school. So I called a strike (this was the 1970s, remember, when everyone was on strike), and after three hours marching around the playground with homemade signs declaring "We want sandwiches," we won. We were allowed to bring sandwiches for lunch. Results! I ran home that night to tell my mom the good news, omitting the bit about me being the ringleader. She listened, then said, "Some people may be bringing sandwiches for lunch, Mark, but you will be having a hot meal every day at school."

So on the first day of the new regime, I was unfortunately at the front of the line facing Mrs. Thomas, who was the nice lunch lady. (The others made my life worse, but Mrs. Thomas was different—she was lovely.) She looked me in the eye and said, "I'm glad you're still with us, Mark. Do you know what would happen if everyone brought sandwiches from home?" "Er, no, Mrs. Thomas," I dutifully replied. "Well, Mark, I wouldn't have a job."

What had I done? It was a tough lesson to learn. But she was right—before long lunchtime staff had halved. It took celebrity chef Jamie Oliver to remedy the situation some three decades later. So, with power, with disruption, comes responsibility. (Sorry, Mrs. Thomas).

The same is true now. You can't run around disrupting stuff willy-nilly. You need to align your disruption with a bigger purpose. (Read David Hieatt's excellent *Do Purpose* to help you define yours.) Having a clear business or personal "Why" really helps here. You've probably seen Simon Sinek's fabulous TED Talk video *Start With Why*, or read the book of the same name, but I make no apologies for recommending that you go and do it again. It is still the best way of defining why what you do matters. Furthermore, having a simple and clear Why allows you to change both your How and your What to build new business ideas. A great Why encourages disruption. A great Why pushes you to find different ways of achieving the same goal. A great Why gives you permission to disrupt.

This isn't just a fanciful approach to business. There are really significant societal changes in the coming years that will affect what we do, how we do it, and even our levels of personal happiness. I'm not going to go into massive detail here, but the power shifts that will have the most impact on our lives over the next fifteen years are as follows:

FROM WEST TO EAST

"Designed in California, Made in China" is what's happening now. The future will be "Designed in China, Made in Africa." The rise of living standards in the Far East means that this market will be the most significant in the world, and will drive trends and consumption. (By 2030, the middle class will have grown by an extra three billion—ten times more than the population of North America and four times more than the EU). It will also see stratospheric growth in the design, business, financial, and service sectors. The West may own these things now, but that won't last. This natural rebalancing of power is here to stay and offers as many opportunities as it does problems. Businesses need to remain nimble and agile in order to survive.

FROM MALE TO FEMALE

This is long overdue and brings with it so many benefits. The old way of working—the tired, aggressive *Apprentice*-inspired way of working—is dead. The broadening of the workforce by gender, most importantly at the top tiers of business, will bring welcome changes to the way we work.

FROM OWNING TO LEASING

I'm not just talking about buying a skydiving experience instead of a smartwatch. I'm talking about changes in how we consume things. The servitization of our economy is happening all around us. Why buy something when you can rent it? Why buy a car when a service plan makes more sense both for you and Ford (since they then keep you as a customer for longer)? Why buy clothes when you can pay one of the fashion retailers a monthly fee to provide you with what you need and then take it back and reprocess it into new clothes for someone else? (Watch this space, it will happen really soon.)

These changes are all around us. They improve things and build on the circular economy principles that will also guide us through resource-scarce times. There will be losers here, however. For example, in the case of cars it will be independent mechanics and second-hand car sales.

They will need to fix other things, become aligned with a larger brand, or sell something else. They will need to change.

FROM PROFESSIONAL TO AMATEUR

The gap between professional and amateur is gone. In the past you'd need a $15,000 editing suite and camera to make broadcast-quality video. Now you need only your iPhone. In the past you'd need a team of web developers to get an online store up and running. Now you need services like Squarespace or Shopify and about three hours. We are all creative. We have democratized media production. This is a good thing (unless your job is now gone—in which case you'd best read this book closely).

PEER-TO-PEER

In the past you'd book a weekend away via a travel agency, stay in a hotel, maybe even rent a car to get there. Now you rent a spare room from someone (Airbnb), eat with the host (who is full of local knowledge), take advice from an online city guide written by people who live there, and maybe use a car-sharing service to drive around, or get an Uber from the station. Travel has changed—this is a biggie, and we are still struggling to work out how to effectively monetize it at scale. But it also presents a big opportunity. How will this affect what you do?

FROM RETAILER TO CONSUMER

We shop with our phones in our hands. Some of us are shopping less. Retail is panicking. What is the product for? Whom is it for? How does it make money? Manufacturers are increasingly bypassing retailers and going direct to customers, as there is a larger profit margin and longer relationships, and the customer gets a better deal too. In ten years, the surviving retailers will be either absolutely brilliant or totally automated.

FROM PEOPLE TO MACHINES

Eek, this one is scary. We are on the edge of an AI revolution. We have started it and we don't know where it will end. This isn't just robots making stuff, this is AI units on your customer care line that can think and make decisions—and you genuinely can't tell whether they're human or not. Some commentators believe that up to 80 percent of our jobs could be replaced by AI. Research firm Gartner predicts that by 2020, 85 percent of our interaction with a brand will not involve a human. That's a worry. Better get thinking.

But this book isn't about thinking. It is about doing. You need to dig out a pencil, carve out a little time, and sit down with the pages that follow.

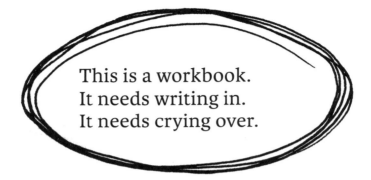

This is a workbook.
It needs writing in.
It needs crying over.

Author Isak Dinesen got it right:

THE CURE FOR ANYTHING IS SALT WATER: SWEAT, TEARS, OR THE SEA.

So, write your name here:

- -

And draw a picture of yourself here:

Don't be shy—it doesn't have to be a good drawing. A stick person will do. Sometimes we forget to draw (as we forget to play), and this is part of creating, of communicating, of telling your story. So pick up a pencil, stick your tongue out of the side of your mouth, concentrate, and draw.

We forget that with every pair of hands comes a free brain. We forget that we have permission to innovate, to disrupt, (If you don't, maybe you're in the wrong job—or maybe that's why you're reading this book.) We forget the big stuff and focus on the small stuff. No one is going to innovate for you. You need to do that. You need to stop blaming time, or key performance indicators, or deadlines, or other people, and get cracking. How are you going to change what you do as a person or as a company to make things better? One of the problems we have is that initiative is not often rewarded. Our culture is to reward compliance. By their very natures innovation and disruption are noncompliant. So the first stage in changing the (your) world is permission. You need to give yourself permission to innovate. You may feel more comfortable asking for permission. That's why one of my mantras is:

ASK FOR FORGIVENESS, NOT PERMISSION.

But this doesn't work for everyone.

It may be that you need to give yourself permission to change. This is more complex. We often find ourselves stuck in a river of thinking due to fear or habit. The key is to break this thinking yourself before it is broken by something else—redundancy, stress, or bankruptcy.

Remember, you have permission to do things differently. In a competitive world, being different is the only thing that makes you stand out. Thinking differently is a competitive advantage.

Once you've given yourself permission to innovate and do things differently, the world looks better. Honestly.

1.
CHANGE

Why do you need to disrupt anything?

Aren't things going swimmingly?

My guess is that you're reading this because you're not happy. Maybe a little not happy. Maybe a lot not happy. The first and most important step is realizing that you're not as happy as you could be. The second is believing that you can change things . . .

. . . if you want to.

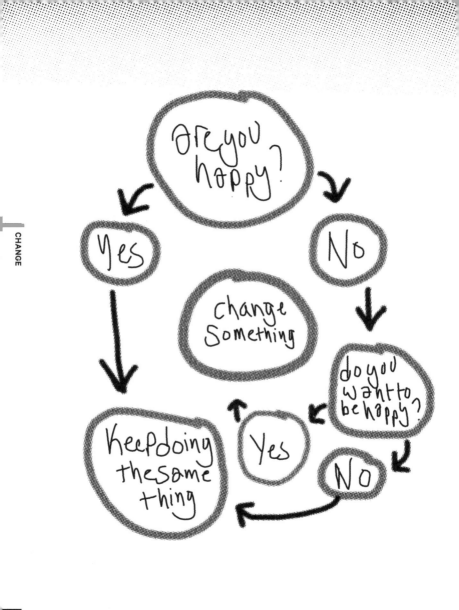

WHAT?

Surely everyone wants
to be happy, right?

Not necessarily.

I know lots of people who aren't happy. Who've been
telling me they're not happy for months. Even years. But
they haven't done anything about it. What do I conclude
from this? That they are happy being unhappy? That they
like the role of moaner in their group of friends?

No, that would be crazy. Wouldn't it? But think about it.
How many people do you know who seem to like being
unhappy? The thing is, staying unhappy is often easier
than changing things to be happy. That takes bravery.

Maybe you're fed up with working for "the man."

I worked for "the man" once.

I won't make that mistake again.

THE MAN

Maybe your ethics don't match your employer's. This is a problem. Your purpose, your moral compass, your beliefs are important. Compromising them makes you unhappy. It's important to do the right thing. We don't leave our core values under our desks when we start work and pick them up when we leave, do we? Well, some do. Do you?

IT'S NOT SUFFICIENT TO DO THINGS BETTER, WE NEED TO DO BETTER THINGS.

Mark Shayler (me)

There are a couple of simple tests here. Think about what you do. Explain it in one sentence.

Write it down here:

Now, what would the twenty-year-old you—the possibly naive, perhaps foolish you, but the essence of you—make of what you do now?

Honestly. Imagine the conversation. How would it go?

Would you be a disappointment to your younger self?

Here's the twenty-year-old me:

The young me would be OK with what I'm doing now but would definitely not have been OK with some of the people I've worked for and the work I've done. This guide from your past will help you move forward.

We start off with high hopes, with a clear vision. But often these hopes get tarnished and our vision becomes less clear. We can spend twenty years becoming good at the wrong thing, climbing the wrong mountain.

The wrong mountain.

The right mountain.

Some of you may be too close to twenty, or may even be under twenty. Hey, that's not a problem. Use your older mentors. Use your grandparents. What would they say about what you do? Would it make them proud?

Here's my Nan and Pap:

Older people often have a different perspective. They know that being famous for selling computers isn't important, and that doing great things and improving the quality of your relationships are. Proximity to death brings much clarity.

And here's the thing:

We don't know when death will come.

It's tempting to put off change. To leave it until later. I coach people in business and I hear this a lot: "When I retire I'm going to give something back/do the thing I always dreamed of." I call this "life-offset." It goes something like this: You spend forty years doing something you don't love so that you can spend five years doing something you've always wanted to do. My advice is to reverse it.

But sometimes it's hard to work out what you want to do. We all have a feeling that there's something waiting for us. It's frustrating to watch time tick past. But remember that there are two types of time: Chronos and Kairos. Chronos is one of the Greek concepts of time. It refers to the linear, measurable flow of seconds, minutes, hours, days, weeks, months, and years. My friend Dave brought Chronos into sharp focus after I remarked how great the past summer was. "Enjoy it; you've probably got only another forty," he said. Yep, I thought, and I'll be incontinent for the last ten. This is the trap of Chronos time: It feels like it is running out.

Think instead about the other concept of time: Kairos. Kairos means the right or opportune moment. You may have run out of Chronos time but have loads of perfect moments left. Sometimes the time is right for doing great things and sometimes it isn't. But you can start thinking about that stuff now. In fact, there is only one time to begin thinking and that is . . .

NOW

Here's a little exercise
to underline why.

Take a disposable tape measure.

I like to keep a couple of spares from IKEA.

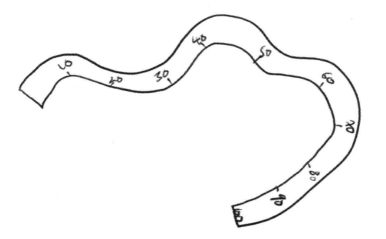

Cut it at your age—for me it's 48.

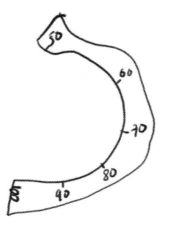

Now cut it again at your likely death age. (Family history will help you here.) Scary, huh?

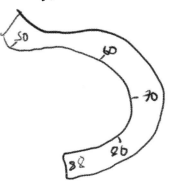

Now cut it again at when you expect to retire.*

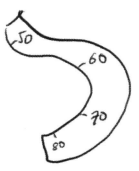

* I've got four kids; I may never retire.

So that's what I've got left.

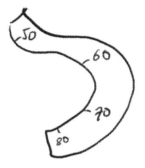

And I'll spend a third of this time sleeping.

Better get cracking then.

YOU'LL REGRET ONLY THE THINGS THAT YOU DON'T DO.

PEOPLE SAY TIME EQUALS MONEY.

THEY'RE WRONG.

IT'S MUCH MORE IMPORTANT THAN THAT.

As singer Jessie J says, "It's not about the money."

If you were solely interested in money, you wouldn't be reading this. Money is important—we all need to live and we all need to earn—but earning it the right way is important.

Mickey Smith (a Do Lectures speaker from 2011) says in his film *Dark Side of the Lens*:

"IF I CAN ONLY SCRAPE A LIVING, AT LEAST IT WILL BE A LIVING WORTH SCRAPING."

These words haunt me. This sense of worth, of purpose, of value is missing from many lives. Time to change that.

Of course you may not want to
change the world. That may not
be your bag. And that's cool
(but it's getting warmer).

It might be that you're just bored
doing what you do. So you need
to change it.

Or you may love what you do and whom you do it for. But you want to do something great in that role. Or you may be returning to a job you don't like. Or you may have "retired" and don't want to retire. As the band The Enemy says, "I'm sick, sick, sick and tired of working just to be retired."

So don't.

DO SOMETHING YOU LOVE.

The key thing is that you want to change something, to make it better. This starts with your Why. Why do you get up in the morning? Why do you carry on breathing? What do you believe in? Write down your Why in the box below. When writing your Why, start with "I believe . . ." and then write down the thing you want to change.

I believe . . .

Elvis didn't want to be a singer.
He wanted to change music. If you're
going to have a dream, have a bloody
big one. We all have a little Elvis in
us. Time to let him out.

Try to let out the pre–Las Vegas Elvis,
with less deep-fat frying involved.

My good friend the designer
James Victore says, "The things
that made you weird as a kid make
you great today." This is true.
Find that weirdness and amplify it.
Bland is dead.

2.
DISRUPT

WHY DISRUPT?

Why not shake ever so gently?

The thing with shaking gently is that you will get only gentle change. Disruptors win. Companies that change markets boom. Great leaps forward come from big external kicks to the market. There are loads of examples of companies who forgot to disrupt, to innovate. Companies that saw their markets disappear. Overnight.

SONY
MISSED
THE MP3.

Coke and Pepsi missed energy drinks.
Hoover missed cyclone technology.
Kodak missed digital.
Nokia forgot about innovation.
Travel agents didn't see the internet.
Decca missed the Beatles.
Borders missed ebooks.
Numerous retailers forgot about customer care.

Large organizations are not able to disrupt.

Or, rather, they don't dare to. They have too much to lose. When you have nothing, you have nothing to lose—hence smaller and younger businesses are much better placed to disrupt. Even pressure groups (usually very disruptive) suffer from this. Once Greenpeace became really successful, it took fewer risks. It had too much to lose. It had money and therefore was worth suing if it was too disruptive. It also had a lot of supporters (like shareholders, really) that it didn't want to offend. So growing bigger pushes organizations into the middle of the road.

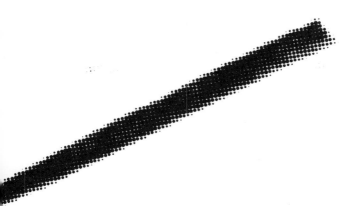

The middle of the road is no place to be, not from a road safety, a music, a creative, or a fashion point of view.

CHANGE HAPPENS AT THE EDGES.

BANDS WHO GET TOO FAMOUS CAN LOSE THEIR EDGE.

They start off all rebellious, all cocky, a bit naive, a bit excitable. They write their first album from this point of view. They write their second while in a hotel room touring the first album. They write their third when they are rich and have lost their hunger. That's why the best bands break up after the first album and why the Rolling Stones should have stopped years ago. But hang on, hold your horses. What about the Beatles?

Some of their best work came later. (*Revolver* is a particular favorite of mine.) There will always be bands (or organizations) that continue to innovate. The secret is that they ensure they've got fresh stimuli: new people, ideas, and even "meditation" to push things on.

Large companies know this, so they employ agencies to be "hungry" for them, or they buy up small hungry companies who change things. That's why Colgate bought Tom's of Maine, Coca-Cola bought Innocent, Unilever bought Ben & Jerry's, Cadbury bought Green & Black's, Timberland bought Howies, and Avis bought Zipcar.

If they can't be disruptive, they buy someone who is. The irony here is that these small disruptive companies have generally stopped being disruptive by then.

All my large clients ask me how they can think like a startup. This needs creative leadership, the right people, the right brief, and constraints.

CONSTRAINTS FIRE INNOVATION.

3.
REBEL INSIDE

Companies spend years and a lot of money creating a culture specific to them. This aids unity and can be an effective representation of brand and personality. However, it can also produce a sterile environment and "groupthink." In that environment it takes a lot of bravery to stand out and do things differently. Ironically, the companies I work with all bemoan this blandness that they've created and find themselves looking for eccentrics and free-thinkers to move things forward.

Often the best and most practical place to innovate is from within a big business. You don't need to buy a ping-pong table and create a startup to do the thing you love. You can build this within the safety of a large organization.

This is how Flickr started. Creating this kind of internal innovation is how Unilever grew the Republic of Axe and was part of the inspiration for their Foundry platform for startups. Similarly, leading UK supermarket Tesco created the highly successful Amplify program to identify and encourage innovative members of their team to grow great ideas.

Developing great ideas inside a bigger business affords you safety and scale. There is a reduced financial risk (maybe this reduces hunger, maybe it doesn't), there are available resources to help you grow, and there is a framework giving you the ability to scale. One big negative is that you won't own the thing you're building (or at least not all of the thing). But this kind of innovation, or intrapreneurship, suits some people and is often a more practical option.

Amazon founder Jeff Bezos talks about how he has created a culture hospitable to experimentation. But it must start on a small scale. His "two-pizza rule" means that if the innovation team needs to order more than a couple of pizzas, it's too big.

The key ingredients to developing ideas inside a big company are:

1. A gnarly challenge. Is there a big challenge or need that you can focus on? Can this solve a problem of the host business and give you the freedom to play?

2. Dedicated time. Are you able to carve out some specific time to work on this? Can you build space into the day to do it properly?

3. Focus. You need extreme focus. Focus on the one thing you want to do.

4. Creative constraint. Constraint creates innovation. Set unrealistic deadlines. Give yourself small budgets. Work in a small team.

5. Accelerated pace. Work fast. Experiment quickly and get to market faster. Being embedded within a larger organization can provide a greater range of resources, which can speed things up. However, the permissions and hurdles you often need to negotiate can be a massive brake on innovation; work with your boss to remove them.

So, working for another company needn't be a barrier to developing new ideas and furthering your own progress, but you need to find a way to work with the strengths of the organization—without losing sight of what you're being paid to do.

YOU NEED TO DISRUPT.

➡️ You need to think.
Thinking is good.
Ideas are what make us tick
(and tock).

Good ideas make your heart beat faster (boom) and take all the air out of the room. So you need ideas. But having the idea is the easy thing. I invented hard disc recorders for video in 1987; I just had no way of making them. An idea is nothing without delivery.

This book will help you make your ideas real. The thing is, you can already do this—you just need a hand to hold. (Choose the left one.)

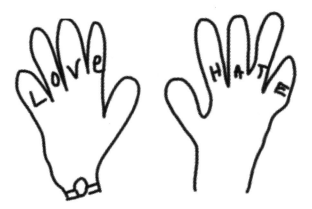

YOU'LL HAVE TO DO SOME WORK TOO.

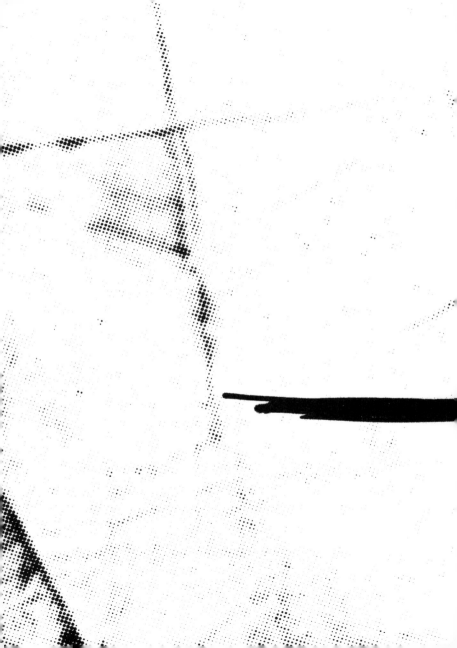

4.
THE BIG
IDEA

SO WHAT'S YOUR IDEA THEN?

Maybe you don't have one yet. The first exercise looked at what you love to do. If that already gave you an idea, don't skip over this section but stay with me for a bit longer—it won't hurt to go over this stuff. When you turn the page, you'll see three columns with titles:

Things you like doing
Things you care about
Things you are good at

Spend some time filling them in.
Be honest; you're defining your purpose here.

Things you are good at

Things you care about

Things you like doing

You've listed your passions, your skills, and the things that give you pleasure. Now I want you to spend a half hour thinking about how these could all come together. Think about some crazy stuff and some boring stuff, then list them on the next page.

MY BIG LIST OF POSSIBLE IDEAS

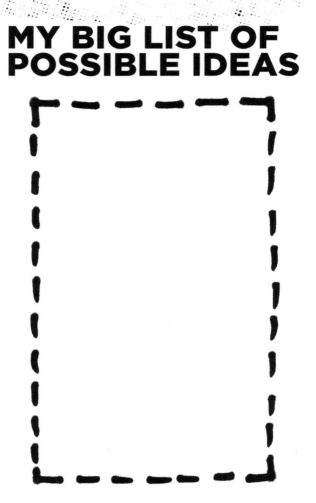

How was that? Too difficult? A bit forced? OK, that's cool.
This next exercise might help. Follow the steps and you
will end up with at least four possible ideas.

IDEA GENERATOR

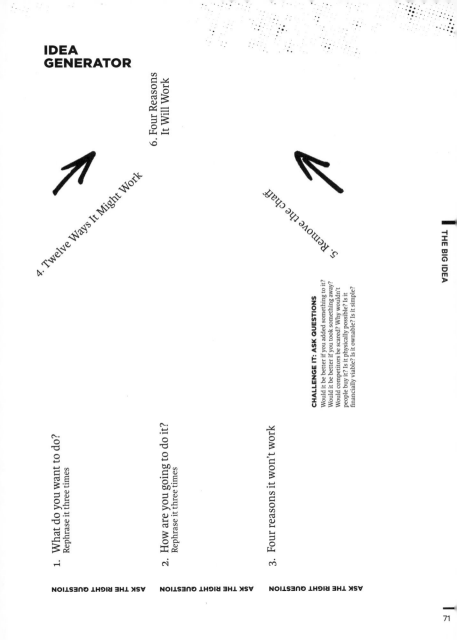

4. Twelve Ways It Might Work

6. Four Reasons It Will Work

5. Remove the chaff

1. What do you want to do?
Rephrase it three times

2. How are you going to do it?
Rephrase it three times

3. Four reasons it won't work

CHALLENGE IT: ASK QUESTIONS
Would it be better if you added something to it?
Would it be better if you took something away?
Would competitors be scared? Why wouldn't
people buy it? Is it physically possible? Is it
financially viable? Is it ownable? Is it simple?

ASK THE RIGHT QUESTION   **ASK THE RIGHT QUESTION**   **ASK THE RIGHT QUESTION**

So you've got your list.

You now need to decide what you want to focus on.

I can't help you here. This will be a combination of passion, maybe income potential, maybe ease of execution. A simple way to look at it is to make a list of the positives and negatives of each idea. There's a template on the opposite page.

It may help to think how you would feel if you couldn't do that thing again. If it hurts to think about it like that, that's the idea you should pursue.

Positives | Negatives

THE BIG IDEA

So that's what you want to do!
(You may have started this book
already knowing that, but it's
good to reconfirm it.)

Now, here's a good bit of advice:

Avoid all business jibberish.
Words like "robust." "Sustainable."
"Paradigm shift." Use simple English.
Don't try to confuse people with
wordy nonsense that doesn't mean
anything. Use as few words as possible.
Turn the page and write down your
idea in the simplest way possible.

Would your grandmother understand it? Would your kids (or grandkids) understand it? If not, do it again.

Now I want you to draw your idea.
Real or symbolic, I don't mind.
Yes, it's that drawing thing again—
but you don't need to be artistic.
It just helps to simplify your thinking.

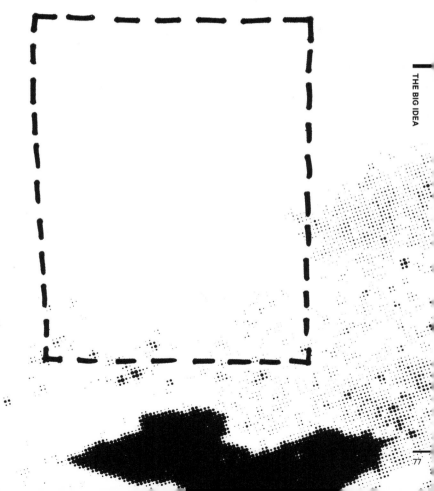

THE BIG IDEA

Have you thought about what a good job looks like for you? This could be quite traditional, like "Achieving a turnover of $250k by year three" or maybe it's more qualitative, like "To be known for making the longest-lasting shoes in the world."

It's probably good to get a balance of the two.

On the next page, write down your quantitative aims and your qualitative aims to help define your vision.

What does a good job look like for you quantitatively (money, sales, that sort of thing)?

And qualitatively (happiness, life balance, that sort of thing)?

Do these aims frighten you?
Are they ambitious enough?
Are they difficult to achieve?
If you answer "no" to any of these,
do the exercise again.

It's good to be scared. Your dreams
should scare you.

Will they make you happy?

Will they make a difference?

What about skills? Do you have all the skills you need to start to bring your Big Idea to life? I don't mean formal education.Everyone knows that degrees don't necessarily equip us with the skills we may need. Online video tutorials and digital tools are out there and available to us all. We can all teach ourselves to build a basic website, shoot an amateur video, and create a simple design or logo for free.

What skills do you need to meet your vision, to make your product or service, to make your customers love you?

Write down your Haves and Needs in two columns on the following page.

Haves | Needs

Consider how you are going to develop these skills yourself, or find people who have them.

DON'T BE AFRAID TO EMPLOY PEOPLE BETTER THAN YOU.

As graphic designer Anthony Burrill says, "Work hard and be nice to people."

No one likes a nastypants.

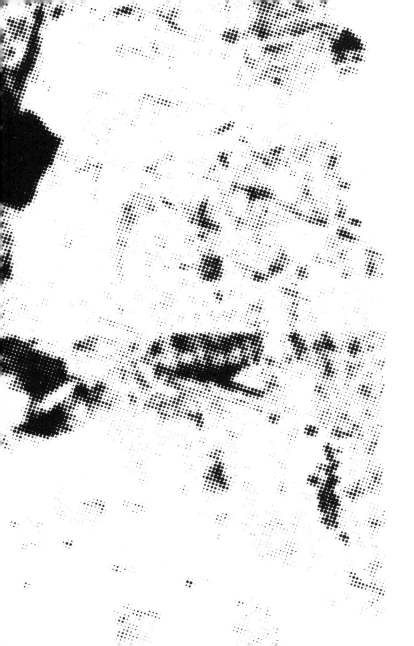

5.
THE
MARKET

So here you are. In your bedroom, shed, office, shower, with a great idea burning a hole in your head.

your idea

And you need to get here:

Success!

(However you define it.)

You need a plan of sorts. Some would even call it a strategy. The diagram below illustrates the typical roller coaster you'll go through when you're trying to make your idea a reality (moving from bottom to top.)

Success!

Bank of Hell!

BANK

Swamp of despair

Mountains of Mayhem

Jungle of Apathy

your Idea

The word "strategy" may sound a bit middle-management, but the concept is useful. Honest.

You aren't going to outspend your competitors, so you'll have to outthink them.

When Ben and Jerry started selling ice cream, they quickly attracted the attention of a big competitor (yep, that one), who bought up all the frozen distribution in the United States, which meant the boys couldn't get their lovely ice cream out of Vermont. They couldn't afford to take this company to court, so instead they started a protest hotline (most calls came in between midnight and 3 a.m.), a T-shirt campaign, a radio campaign, and a bus poster campaign. Guess what?

They won. The big company backed down. Brains, not money, was the victor.

So this would be a great time to list your competitors. And remember, it's OK to like your competitors!

Now, what about thinking a bit broader? Think about how your competitors' products make people feel. Where else can consumers buy that feeling? That's also your competition. Look at that: you've reduced the risk of missing competition emerging from your blind spot.

Broader competitors:

What do you admire about your competitors?

Now think about why people might stop using your competitors' product or service and start using yours. What do they have to lose? What do they have to gain? Why will your product be a knockout?

Grateful Dead front man Jerry Garcia once said,

"YOU DO NOT MERELY WANT TO BE CONSIDERED JUST THE BEST OF THE BEST. YOU WANT TO BE CONSIDERED THE ONLY ONES WHO DO WHAT YOU DO."

Now, I want you to think about your unfair advantage. I want you to think about what you have that no one else has. I want you to try to articulate that in a sentence. Then I want you to list five ways a consumer will benefit by using your idea. Be specific. Avoid vague words like "quality," "value," and "reliability."

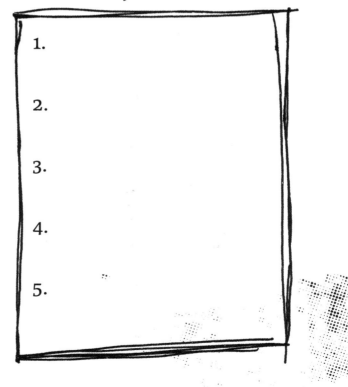

1.

2.

3.

4.

5.

Once you have your great idea that offers something different to the market, you need to identify your market.

Who will pay money for your product or service?

Define your customer.

You can't say simply "people like me."

That's lazy.

Who is your customer? Think about things like age, education, and hobbies. Where do they shop? What do they do in their free time? What brands do they associate with? Write this stuff in the space below. Maybe draw another stick figure.

I'm going to ask you to do some cutting and pasting now. Don't shy away from this one; it's really useful. First, run around the house/doctor's waiting room/newsstand and take as many magazines as you can. (Please pay for them first.) Then, cut out people, places, things, and activities that relate to your customer, and use the clippings to create a photo collage of their lives. Think about their families, houses, possessions, kids, cars, jobs, pets. Don't hold back. This exercise helps build a detailed picture of both the customer and the context.

I've done this exercise with hundreds of clients. After a few minutes' resistance they really get into it. There's nothing better than seeing company executives and directors on their hands and knees cutting and pasting. There's also nothing better than going back to the same client six months later and seeing the collage on the wall, still being modified, still being used.

Once you've identified your market, it's also worth looking at the flip side. Who is *not* your customer? Who do you need to convert to buy from you? Who *should* want your products but doesn't know about them yet? Who thinks they are too young, too old, too whatever to use your products?

List them below.

Now let's look at what your customers are really buying. What do I mean? I mean that even if they'll eventually be buying your product (hopefully), they might be currently getting the same utility, and possibly the same feeling, from some other source. It's worth thinking about this a little.

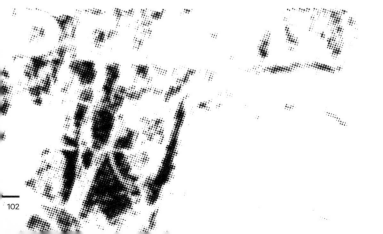

Suppose you sell bikes. People buy bikes for a number of reasons. They buy them as a leisure or sports activity, or a form of transport, or a way of losing weight or getting fit, or having time alone to think.

So, as a bike seller you are not competing just with other bike sellers but with companies who sell exercise machines, cars, fishing rods, running shoes, meditation classes, and gyms.

How else can your customers get the benefits that your product or service provides?

What are you really selling?

What benefits are you selling?

Your customers are exposed to highly sophisticated branding.

Their expectations are high.

Remember this.

You need to be really good.

YOU NEED TO BE DIFFERENT.

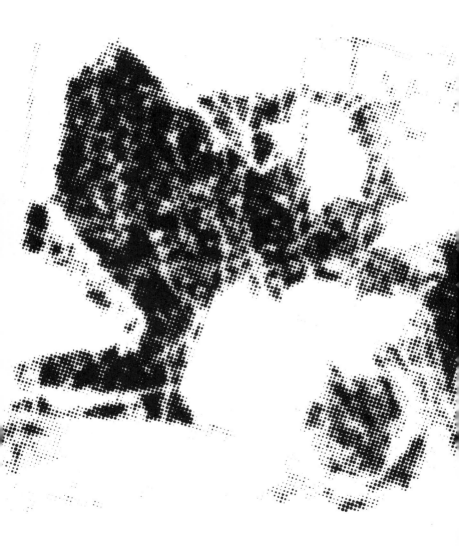

6.
INNOVATE

So you've identified your competition and worked out who your customers are. How will you offer them something truly different?

Innovation isn't something you should hire outsiders to come in and do for you, because once they've helped you, they are on to the next job and your business is in danger of stagnating again. The secret is to build a culture of innovation inside your organization (even if it is an organization of one). This way, you will always be innovating, always be thinking of new ways of doing things.

Key skills here are observation and thoughtfulness. Sit with the problem longer. Be a bit Buddhist about it all. Get comfortable with taking in information and letting it roll around in your head. It's a fundamental skill of designers, innovation experts, and anyone wanting to grow their business.

So how do you innovate?

For some it's a natural thing,
while others need a process in
place. Innovation processes are
a dime a dozen, and there's one
out there for you.

Here is the one I use:

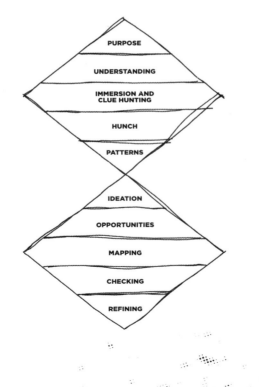

PURPOSE

UNDERSTANDING

IMMERSION AND
CLUE HUNTING

HUNCH

PATTERNS

IDEATION

OPPORTUNITIES

MAPPING

CHECKING

REFINING

Start with a focused question. For example, How can we build a better table? Then go as wide as possible to understand the brief and look for clues. Be disruptive, asking things like "Why don't we all eat with bibs?" Then narrow in and focus on hunches and patterns. From there, develop ideas and go as wide as possible again. These ideas generate opportunities, which in turn are then mapped and checked for relevance. Finally, the shaping and refining begins. Most innovation processes are similar.

But it's not the process that delivers. It's the people involved. Always.

We are all different. Some of us like to schedule ideas sessions, some of us like to meditate to come up with great ideas, some like to work in a group, some like to work alone. It doesn't matter, as long as it works for you. Here are some ways of thinking about it that have been successful for me:

1. Someone once said we are the average of the five people we spend the most time with. Want to think differently? Spend time with people who see things differently.

2. If you want a better answer, ask a better question. When a well-known manufacturer of spray-on deodorant wanted to sell 20 percent more product, the solution they (or their design agency) came up with was to make the hole that the spray came out of 20 percent bigger. Bonkers. A better question would have been "How do we make 20 percent more profit?" The answer in this case might be to make the hole 20 percent *smaller*, thereby decreasing the amount of product labeled as "one application." If they make this change but keep the price the same, they end up with not only a 20 percent increase in profit but also reduced manufacturing costs and packaging waste, and fewer delivery trucks on the road (not to mention less wasted product by consumers who would otherwise use more than they need).

3. Better people make better businesses, and better businesses make a better world. At the heart of this is you. Look after yourself. Sleep well. Drink lots of water. Meditate. Do yoga. Run. Ride a bike. Go to the gym. Eat well. Reduce sugar and sweeteners. You know this stuff already.

4. Consider your surroundings. Where do you have your best ideas? At a desk? Unlikely. Get out of the office and into your element. Also, don't call it an office. Call it a studio. If you work in an office you will push paper. If you work in a studio you may create some magic.

5. Keep a scrapbook. Yes, a scrapbook. When you see things you like, photograph them, print them, and stick them in it. There is something lovely about a physical book like this. Yes, you could use Pinterest or Pocket and myriad other apps and tools. But nothing beats paper for collecting and annotating ideas.

6. You probably already have the right people inside your organization to generate awesome ideas. (Try the process on page 110.) Trust them. Find the rebels inside your company and work with them.

7. Use the "sprint" method, from Jake Knapp's book of the same name. (See the Resources section at the back of this book for more info.) When I'm working with one of my side projects, Rebel Cell, we use sprints and hacks to get stuff done quickly and well. Sprint methodology is simple and effective.

Above all, you've got to . . .

. . . keep your radar on. Always.

It is all about observation. Take your earphones out. Walk instead of taking the subway. Ride your bike instead of driving your car. Keep your eyes open.

THE BEST INNOVATIONS SOLVE PROBLEMS THAT PEOPLE DIDN'T KNOW EXISTED.

You need to identify insights.

The challenge is to distinguish between valuable insights and valueless insights. We all spot things people are doing; the tough thing is understanding what is just a fad and what can lead to wider-scale change.

In a world where the web makes it easy for us to see trends, the trends themselves become less important. Being able to draw insights, however, from trends can give you a competitive advantage.

How do you identify insights?
Where do you look? How often?
Do you use trend-spotting websites,
read contemporary journals, talk
to customers? Watch people? Write
them down here:

Here's an example. VF Corporation (the owners of Lee and Wrangler) observed that women didn't enjoy buying jeans. In fact, women rated buying jeans as the second-most intimidating clothes shopping experience. Cuts were confusing. Vanity sizing didn't help. Jeans were poorly displayed. In response, VFC simplified sizing and cuts, changed displays and communication, and saw a $100 million increase in revenue.

(Story from Scott Anthony's *The Little Black Book of Innovation*.)

THE SECRET IS TO PREDICT WHAT YOUR CUSTOMER WANTS BEFORE THEY KNOW. HERE'S A HANDFUL OF SIMPLE WAYS TO DO THIS.

Spend time with people to identify their problems, needs, and opportunities. What need is your idea addressing?

→ Watch for workarounds. People will shortcut badly designed products and services, and develop their own process. Spot these and BINGO!

→ Don't restrict your thinking to your known market. There will be hundreds of people out there who love what you have to offer. They just don't know about it yet.

So how are you going to tell people about the super-duper product or service you've made?

We all know that routes to market have changed. The internet rules, yes? Well, that's true, but the internet is a big place and you're quite small.

It can be a bit like . . .

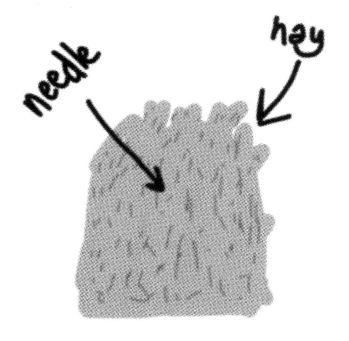

needle

hay

To get noticed, you will need to create a bit of a stir and build your tribe.

What are your planned routes to market? How are you going to get heard above the noise? Sometimes talking to customers in a different way is enough to get their attention. Sometimes you need to do the opposite of your competitors. Sometimes use social media, sometimes traditional media.

The gap between professional and amateur has shrunk. You can teach yourself to write great blog posts without a degree in journalism, compose great copy without a background in copywriting, take great photographs with your iPhone, and produce great video at home. Just do it.

So how are people going to find out about you? About how great you are? You don't want to keep it a secret. Start by writing some ideas here:

7.
DETAILS

It's about time we considered the issue of money. How much do you need to cover your costs? (Don't forget to include a salary for you—a more common mistake than you think.) How much of your product or service do you need to sell to break even? What's the profit per unit? What if costs rise? What will you do before that point? Do you need investors? If so, how much do you need from them? Can you take advantage of R&D tax credits or other innovation incentives?

I know it's boring, but it's important.

Great ideas are often derailed by poor cash-flow and tricky financial stuff.

So get it right.

Spend some time coming to grips with the numbers. But don't lose your vision. Remember: There are ways of making the numbers work if you want something badly enough.

Now we're getting somewhere.

It's time to do a SWOT analysis. "Oh great," I hear you say. "A bloody SWOT analysis." Don't scoff. These things may be a bit basic, but they work. So stop whining and get the Strengths, Weaknesses, Opportunities, and Threats written down. Be honest. Think about what we've looked at so far: the market, competitors, customers, cash flow, skills (or lack of), and so on. Off you go! ➤

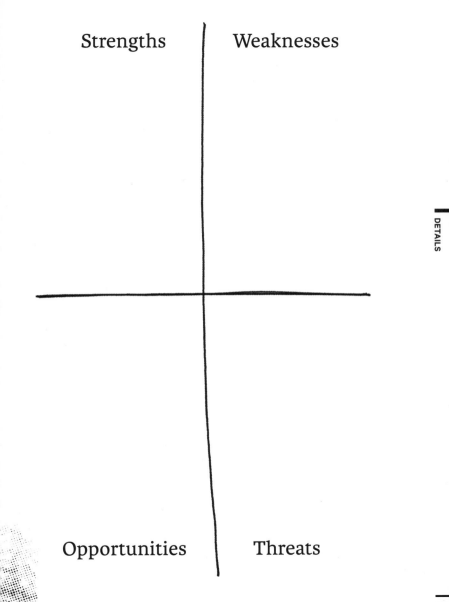

Strengths   Weaknesses

Opportunities   Threats

Ideally you want more things written down on the left-hand side of the page than the right. But don't be dismayed if you haven't.

Now, for each Opportunity, Weakness, and Threat, I want you to write three actions. ➡

For each Strength, I want you to punch the air enthusiastically, whoop and holler—or just give yourself a little self-satisfied smile.

ACTION POINTS

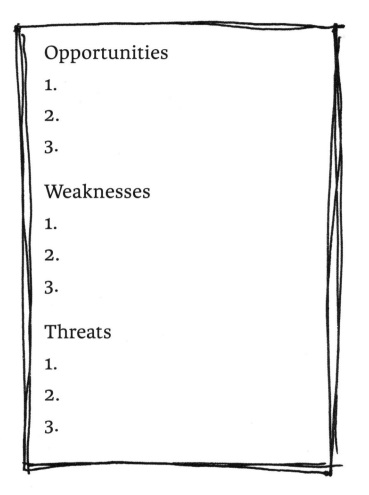

Opportunities

1.

2.

3.

Weaknesses

1.

2.

3.

Threats

1.

2.

3.

OK. That's all been good. All lovely and straightforward. Now I want to focus on the things that are stopping you from being awesome. On the opposite page, list all the things that you think stand in the way of you being brilliant.

PERCEIVED BARRIERS

I'm not sure I can do this because . . .

The next bit is dead simple:

Identify.

Remove.

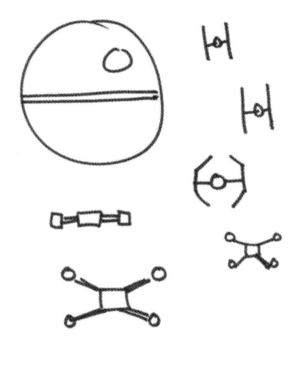

So, to summarize, you've worked out if you want to be happy, had a word with the twenty-year-old you, had a chat with your grandma, done some drawing, generated some ideas, measured your life line with a tape measure, done some more drawing, defined what a good job looks like, defined your customer, looked at what you're really selling, written down your haves and needs, looked at insights and innovation, listed five benefits you can offer customers, planned the routes to market, written an action plan, and identified and removed things stopping you.

And you got your head straight and resolved to start.

There is only one thing left.

GO
AND
DO.

May the force be with you.

Resources

Books

Tools of Titans, Tim Ferris, Vermilion (2016)

Ego Is the Enemy, Ryan Holiday, Profile Books (2016)

The Future Book, Magnus Lindkvist, LID Publishing (2015)

The Pirate Inside, Adam Morgan, John Wiley & Sons (2004)

Sprint: How to Solve Big Problems and Test New ideas in Just Five Days, Jack Knapp, John Zeratsky, and Braden Kowitz, Bantam Press (2016)

Unboss, Lars Kolind and Jacob Bøtter, Jyllands-Postens Forlag (2012)

It's Not How Good You Are, It's How Good You Want To Be, Paul Arden, Phaidon Press Ltd (2003)

Do Purpose, David Hieatt, Do Books (2010)

Consumed: How Shopping Fed the Class System, Harry Wallop, Collins (2013)

Podcasts

Mind Your Business, James Wedmore and Phoebe Mroczek

Longform, Aaron Lammer, Max Linsky, and Evan Ratliff

Distraction Pieces, Scroobius Pip

Start Up, Alex Blumberg and Lisa Chow

Revisionist History, Malcolm Gladwell

Websites

FastCompany.com

Wired.com

TrendHunter.com

SethGodin.typepad.com

TheDoLectures.com

About the Author

Mark Shayler runs Ape, an innovation-sustainability-brand agency. He has worked with some of the world's largest and smallest businesses, including Amazon, Samsung, Coca-Cola, Unilever, and John Lewis, saving them shed-loads* of carbon, increasing sales by more than 6,000 percent, and helping develop new products and services. He is also a cofounder of Rebel Cell, where he builds startups inside of larger organizations, and a founding partner of the Do Lectures.

He keeps ducks, chickens, and children (all free-range), and makes fantastic smoked chile sauce. He follows the usual middle-aged pursuits of playing on bikes and making sourdough bread. He is a Virgo who will never get over failing to play professional rugby and not being the lead singer of an indie rock band. But there's still time and nothing is impossible.

* Technical term.

© Simon Edwards

Thanks

Thanks go to my folks and brother, Guy, who gave me a happy childhood; my kids (Daisy, Max, Tilly, and Moo) for being fantastic, keeping me young, and starting their own ventures; and Nicola for being my true love. Thanks also to Miranda West for being a top publisher, and to David and Clare Hieatt for starting the Do Lectures and being great friends. Thanks to top-drawer designer Anthony Oram for making this book look great. In my early life I was lucky enough to have a couple of amazing teachers who made me feel that I could achieve anything and engaged me with stories and tales that quickened my pulse. So hats off to Mr. Day, Mr. Spencer, Miss Dalton, and the late Mr. Woodward. A big manly hug for the best boss I ever had, Dai Larner. Thanks also to the inspirational Do community, all of you, and to my team at Ape.

Notes

:DO:

Books in the series:

Do Fly
Find your way. Make a living.
Be your best self.
Gavin Strange

Do Grow
Start with 10 simple vegetables.
Alice Holden

Do Story
How to tell your story so the world listens.
Bobette Buster

A percentage of royalties from each copy sold will go to the DO Lectures, a workshop series for sharing ideas and inspiring action.

For more in the DO Books series, visit **www.chroniclebooks.com.**

To learn more about DO Lectures, visit **www.thedolectures.com.**